indoor gardening

Cameron and Margaret Yerian, Editors

 CHILDRENS PRESS, CHICAGO

Executive Editors
Cameron John Yerian, M.A.
Margaret A. Yerian, M.A.

Art Director
Thomas Petiet, M.F.A.

Designer
Cameron John Yerian

Senior Editor
Mary Rush, M.F.A.
Sharon Irvine, B.A.

Contributors
Nancy Muhlbach, M.A.
Jerry Gillmore, B.A.
Mary White, B.A.
Edith Wolter, B.S.
Susan Keezer
Virginia Foster, A.B.

Editorial Assistant
Phoebe A. Yerian

Readability Consultants
Donald E.P. Smith, Ph.D.
School of Education
University of Michigan

Judith K. Smith, Ph.D.
University of Michigan

Instructional Development Consultant
Joel B. Fleming, M.A.
Instructional Development & Technology
Michigan State University

Synectics Consultant
Gershom Clark Morningstar, M.A.
President, Wolverine-Morningstar Media

Library Consultant
Noel Winkler, M.A.L.S.
Lecturer, Children's Literature
Elementary Librarian, Media Center
School of Education
University of Michigan

Library of Congress Cataloging in Publication Data
Main entry under title:

Indoor gardening.

   (Fun time activities)
   Includes index.
   SUMMARY: Advice for the indoor gardener on such
generalities as potting, watering, and propagating and
on such specific plants as pineapple, avocado, and
Boston fern.
   1. House plants—Juvenile literature. 2. Glass
gardens—Juvenile literature. [1. House plants]
I. Yerian, Cameron John. II. Yerian, Margaret.
SB419.15   635.9′65   75-15781
ISBN 0-516-01323-8

1 2 3 4 5 6 7 8 9 10 11 12 R 80 79 78 77 76 75

Contents

CARE & TRAINING 5

Pot & Repot 6
Dirty Mix-Up 7
Rain Maker 8
Eggs for Lunch 10
Bathing Your Beauties 11
Root of the Matter 12

MORE THAN BEFORE 13

Lucky Leaf 14
Disappearing Stripes 15
Violet Vim 15
Tip Slips 16
Cut Offs 17
Up in the Air 18
Send a Runner 20
The Great Divide 21
Crazy Carrot 22
Boastful Beet 23
Pokey Pineapple 24
Amazing Avocado 25
Outcast Onion 26
Sneaky Sweet Potato 27
Root of the Matter 28

PORTABLE GARDENS 29

Carrot Basket 30
Wet Feet 32
Bashful Basket 33
Herb Ins & Outs 34
Miniscape 36
Caring Hints 40
Button Business 41
Dunescape 42
Mountain Magic 44

INDEX 46

CARE, & TRAINING

Pot & Repot

USE clay or plastic pots with drainage holes in the bottom for seedlings and house plants.

SCRUB old pots with a brush and hot soapy water. Rinse them well. Let them dry. Give the new plant a clean start.

SOAK new clay pots a while in plain water before you use them. You should dry them thoroughly too.

CHOOSE small pots for small plants. Start seedlings or slips in them.

PUT pieces of broken pots over the holes in the bottom. Add a layer of gravel or sand for drainage.

FILL the pot with a soil mix. Plant your plant!

REPOT it when you see the roots crawl out the bottom hole. Use a pot just a little bigger than the one before. Flowering plants do better with crowded roots. With too much room they make lots of leaves and forget to bloom.

POTTING SOIL

Dirty Mix-Up

MAKE your own potting soil.

MIX equal amounts of garden soil, dampened peat moss, and perlite. The garden soil contains things to feed the plant. The peat moss holds moisture like a sponge. Perlite (crushed volcanic rock) keeps the soil particles apart so air and water can get through. Vermiculite and sand do this too.

MIX UP a small batch. Try 1 cup of each. Add 1/2 teaspoon of ground limestone and three 1/2 teaspoons of bone meal. Doesn't that sound tasty? Stir it well!

GIVE desert-type plants, like cactus, twice as much perlite and no moss. limestone, or bone meal. They are on a very low-calorie diet.

PUT big plants with fat roots and leaves on a heavier diet. They like lots of garden soil and only a little peat moss and perlite.

Rain Maker

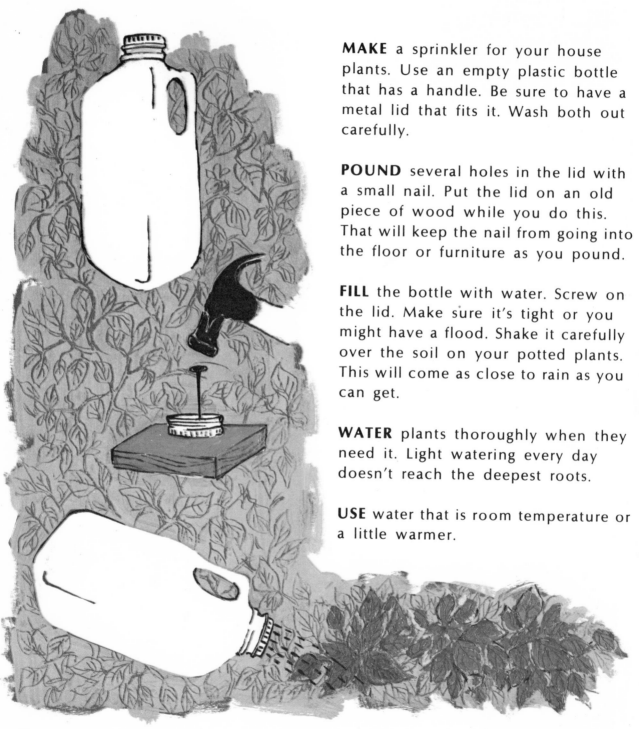

MAKE a sprinkler for your house plants. Use an empty plastic bottle that has a handle. Be sure to have a metal lid that fits it. Wash both out carefully.

POUND several holes in the lid with a small nail. Put the lid on an old piece of wood while you do this. That will keep the nail from going into the floor or furniture as you pound.

FILL the bottle with water. Screw on the lid. Make sure it's tight or you might have a flood. Shake it carefully over the soil on your potted plants. This will come as close to rain as you can get.

WATER plants thoroughly when they need it. Light watering every day doesn't reach the deepest roots.

USE water that is room temperature or a little warmer.

TOUCH the soil to see if it's dry. If it is, get out the sprinkling can.

GIVE each potted plant a drip dish so you don't get moisture rings where it sits. Water some plants from the bottom. Fill the drip dish and let the plant do the rest.

MAKE SURE your plants don't get thirsty when you leave for a weekend. Here are some ways:

BEGIN by watering the plants that need it.

LEAVE water standing in the drip dish under extra thirsty plants.

PUT a plastic bag over your plants. This tent will help keep moisture in.

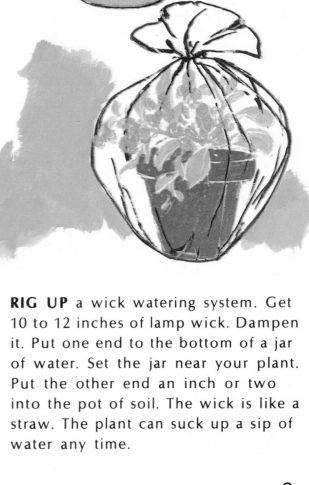

RIG UP a wick watering system. Get 10 to 12 inches of lamp wick. Dampen it. Put one end to the bottom of a jar of water. Set the jar near your plant. Put the other end an inch or two into the pot of soil. The wick is like a straw. The plant can suck up a sip of water any time.

9

Eggs for Lunch

SAVE your egg shells from breakfast to make a healthy lunch for your plants.

SMASH the shells and drop them into a jar of water. Let them stand for three or four days.

STRAIN OFF the water solution. Use it to feed your plants. That should "egg" them on!

LEARN what each plant likes to eat. Some have a sweet tooth and like their soil and food on the alkaline side. Others have sour tastes. Acid soil for them. Some will eat anything.

FIND OUT their eating schedules. They don't all get hungry at the same time. One feeding a month is plenty for most plants. But a few are ravenous. Others can get along without food for several months.

MAKE a feeding chart to keep track of the meals you serve. That way they will all be happy.

Bathing Your Beauties

GET an inexpensive insect spray gun. A sprayer lid, like the ones you find on the top of bottles of window cleaner, will also work.

MAKE SURE it is thoroughly clean. Some plants are very fussy about what is in their bath water. Fill it with lukewarm water.

GIVE the plants a spray bath several times a week. They won't know if it's the dew or you if you keep the spray fine enough.

SPRAY them more often during the months when your house is heated. It will keep their leaves from drying out and turning brown.

USE a sponge, mild soap, and lukewarm water to clean the large leaves on some foliage plants. Philodendrons, palms and ivies need this about once a week. It will keep the openings in their leaves unclogged. Then the plant can breathe freely. Don't you feel good after a nice warm bath?

Root of the Matter

You can make a garden in almost any kind of container. It doesn't need to be fancy. You can make it that way.

Use a clay pot. Use a wooden box. Use a milk carton. Use a plastic pail or an old kitchen sink. Use your head and make a container for your garden from anything you like.

Decorate your container if you want. All it really needs are drainage materials and a friendly place in the sun.

Make your plant home big. Make it little. Just make it go with the size of the plants you want to grow.

Buy a container. Borrow a container. Make a container.

Have it square. Have it round. Have it right side up or upside down.

Get something old. Get something new. The home is for the garden. And the garden's for you.

MORE
than
BEFORE

Lucky Leaf

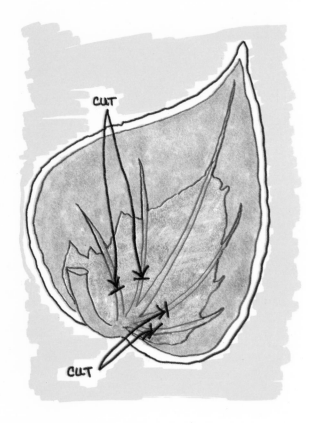

GET a big healthy leaf from a rex begonia in the spring. It needs to have a 1 inch piece of stem left on it.

FIND a box about 9 inches square and 5 inches deep. Make sure it has drainage holes in it. Cover the holes with broken pieces of pots. Fill it with 3 inches of peat moss and sand, mixed.

TURN the leaf upside down on a piece of cardboard on the table. Ask someone older to help you now. Get a sharp knife. Cut through each main vein just below the spot where it branches out.

MAKE a hole in the soil for the stem. Place the leaf right side up flat on the sandy soil. Put the stem in the hole. Press the soil around it.

SLIP the planted box into a clear plastic bag. Close it loosely.

CHECK it every day. Soon each cut vein will grow a new little rex begonia. Remove the plastic. Pot each one when they are big enough to leaf alone.

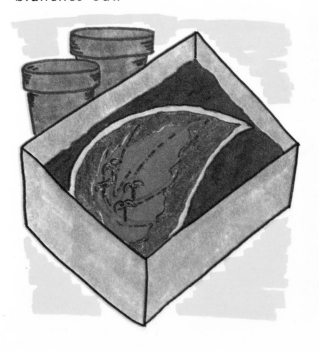

FIND somebody who has a striped snake plant. Ask him if you could have a leaf from it. Cut the leaf into 4 inch pieces. Be sure to keep them right side up.

PUT the bottom 2 inches down into a clean pot filled with a mixture of half sand, half peat moss. Water it lightly.

SLIP the pot into a plastic bag. Close it at the top. Soon a sneaky green snake plant will creep up from below.

LOOK at it! No stripes!

Violet Vim

GET an African violet leaf with a 2 inch stem.

FIX a clean pot with moist rooting mix. Poke a hole. Put in the stem. Firm the mix around it. Put it in a plastic bag.

WAIT! A new plant will grow from the stem.

Tip Slips

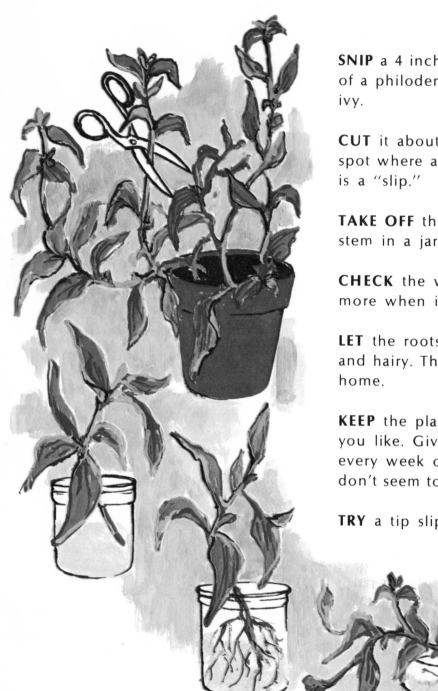

SNIP a 4 inch piece from the tip end of a philodendron, wandering Jew, or ivy.

CUT it about a 1/4 inch below the spot where a leaf joins the stem. This is a "slip."

TAKE OFF the lowest leaves. Put the stem in a jar of water.

CHECK the water level often. Add more when it's needed.

LET the roots on the stem get good and hairy. Then give it a more elegant home.

KEEP the plant growing in water, if you like. Give it a sip of plant food every week or two. These plants don't seem to mind a liquid diet at all.

TRY a tip slip soon.

Cut Offs

GET a window full of winter blooms from one worn-out geranium. Do bring a tired geranium inside that's been blooming outside all summer. Make all new plants from it. They will bloom all winter.

CUT several branches about 5 inches long from the big plant. Trim off the bottom leaves. Keep a few leaves at the top of each cutting. Take off any blooms.

CLEAN a 3 inch pot for each cutting. Put pieces of broken pots over the drainage holes. Fill each pot with a mixture of 1 part sand, 1 part soil, and 1 part peat moss or vermiculite.

POKE a deep hole in the soil of each pot with a stick or your finger. Pour a little sand in the bottom of the hole for good drainage.

PLACE a cutting in each pot. Pat the soil down firmly. Keep them watered. Don't put them in direct sunlight until new leaves appear. That tells you the cuttings have grown roots.

Congratulations! Clear the windowsill!

Up in the Air

FIND a spindly dieffenbachia or rubber plant. Choose a branch to make a new plant from. Try this in the spring. Start at the tip and follow down the stem about a foot until you find a little knob-like bud.

TAKE a sharp knife. Carefully cut to the center of the stem just below that bud. Now turn the knife a little and continue the cut upward for about 2 inches. Easy does it! Bend the branch back a little. Looks a lot like a tongue sticking out at you, doesn't it.

GET a bunch of sphagnum moss. Florists have it. Maybe you can get some from a bait store. They often keep worms in it. You can use crushed straw or hay if you can't get moss.

WET the moss thoroughly. Use rain or pond water if you can. Squeeze it out like a sponge. Put a small piece under the tongue you cut. Tie a little splint of wood to the back side of the cut if it seems to need it.

18

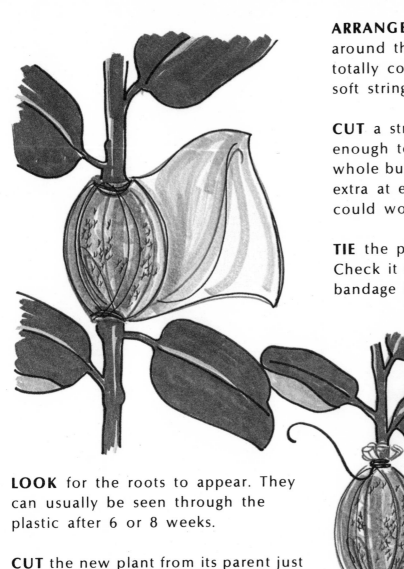

ARRANGE the rest of the moss around the cut area. Make sure it is totally covered. Tie it in place with soft string.

CUT a strip of plastic wrap long enough to wrap twice around the whole bunch of moss. Allow 2 inches extra at each end. Aluminum foil could work too.

TIE the plastic snugly at both ends. Check it every day to make sure the bandage hasn't slipped.

LOOK for the roots to appear. They can usually be seen through the plastic after 6 or 8 weeks.

CUT the new plant from its parent just below the moss root ball. Take off the plastic carefully.

PLANT it in a pot, moss and all.

TRY the same up-in-the-air trick on a juniper or rhododendron in your yard. They might need a little rooting powder on the cut to help things along.

Send a Runner

LOOK for a Boston fern. These send out long thread-like runners from the base of the plant. They really look hairy!

PREPARE a 3 inch pot for planting. Put pieces of broken pot over the drainage holes. Then a little gravel or sand. Top with a standard soil mix of equal amounts of peat moss, perlite, and garden soil.

PUT the pot near the big plant. Help the runner run into it. Stop it in the middle of the pot with a hairpin or maybe a little stone. Keep it watered.

WATCH tiny leaves appear at the tip of the runner. When there are three or four leaves, cut the runner. The new little fern can run on its own.

DISCOVER other plants that put out runners. How about a spider plant, hens and chickens, or even strawberry plants? Let their runners touch soil and you have a new plant.

The Great Divide

FIND a fat fern or a scrunched snake plant that has gotten too big for its own good. Let's help them out before they pop their pots.

LAY the pot on its side. Gently hold the base of the plant. Jiggle it carefully. This should loosen the roots from the pot. If the soil is moist, it will loosen easier.

LOOK at all those tangled roots!

STICK two forks back to back into the middle of the root mess.

GRAB both fork handles and pry the roots apart. You might want to cut the fern roots apart.

DIVIDE the big plant cluster into as many little plants as you can. Plant each one in its own comfortable pot.

Think how much better they must feel!

CRAZY CARROT

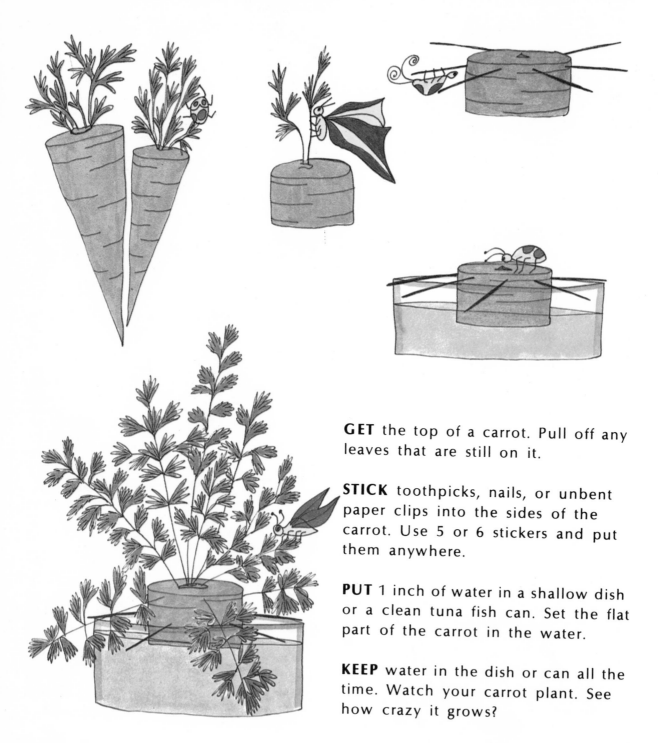

GET the top of a carrot. Pull off any leaves that are still on it.

STICK toothpicks, nails, or unbent paper clips into the sides of the carrot. Use 5 or 6 stickers and put them anywhere.

PUT 1 inch of water in a shallow dish or a clean tuna fish can. Set the flat part of the carrot in the water.

KEEP water in the dish or can all the time. Watch your carrot plant. See how crazy it grows?

Boastful Beet

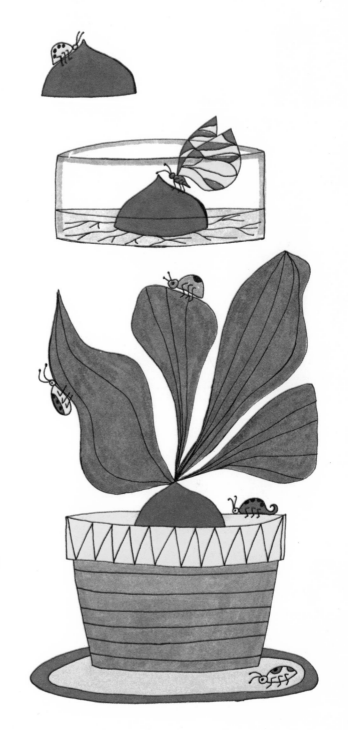

GROW a plant from a beet top. Begin it as you did the carrot. But leave out the toothpicks or nails.

PULL OFF any leaves that are left on the beet. Put the flat part in water.

PLANT the beet in a container of sand when it has roots. You'll have pretty boastful leaves.

DO the same thing but get a different kind of leaf. Use a parsnip instead of a beet.

THINK of other trimmings that will grow into something nice to keep. You'll also be helping the garbage man.

Pokey Pineapple

SAVE the top of a fresh pineapple. Leave about 1/4 inch of fruit around the top.

TAKE OFF the bottom row of leaves. Let your piece of pineapple dry for 2 days.

FIND a dish with low sides. Put an inch of sand in it. Pour on enough water to make the sand damp.

PUSH the pineapple top into the sand. Have the flat end down.

WATER the plant often. Keep it in a warm place but don't let the sun shine right on it.

WAIT until new leaves grow. Then move your plant to a larger home. Use 1 cup of top soil and 2 cups of perlite.

You probably won't get any new fruit. But your pokey leaves will look nice. And if you keep it for a while you might get perky blossoms.

Amazing Avocado

SAVE an avocado seed. Take off the brown coat that looks like paper.

GET a pot with good drainage holes. Fill it with potting soil.

PUSH the flat end of the seed down into the soil. Leave the pointed end sticking up.

START your avocado seed in a dim light. Give it more sunlight a little at a time as it grows.

WATER your seed every day. When the plant begins to grow, keep the soil damp all the time.

TAKE good care of your plant. You may end up with a tree.

Outcast Onion

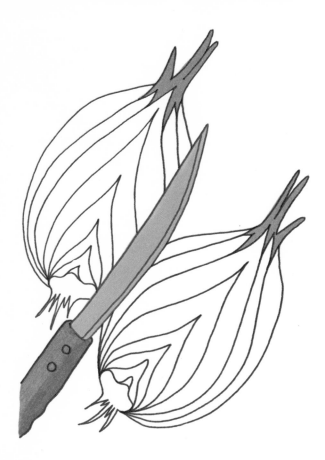

GET two small, yellow onions.

CUT one in half from the top to the bottom. Look at the very center of the onion layers.

CHECK for layers that look like folded leaves. Try to figure out what will happen to these leaves if you plant the onion.

PLANT the other onion in a small pot of soil. Put it about 2 inches under the top of the soil. Set the pot in a dish.

GIVE the pot a spot that is warm and sunny. Keep water in the dish under it.

WATCH your onion plant grow. Where does the sprout come from? Where does an onion keep its food?

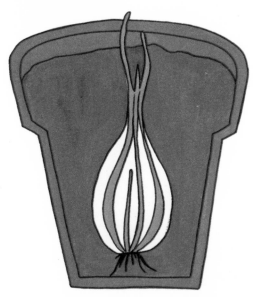

26

Sneaky Sweet Potato

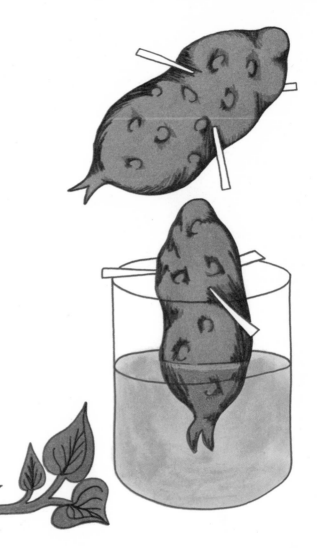

GET a small sweet potato that has not been coated with wax. Try to find one with lively looking eyes.

PUSH 3 toothpicks or nails into the middle of the potato. Leave the same amount of space between each one.

FIND a glass jar that is bigger around than the potato. Fill it half full of water.

REST the toothpicks on the edge of the jar. The bottom of the potato should just touch the water. If the water is higher, pour some out.

SET the jar in a dark place. Give the potato sunlight as it grows. Do it a little at a time.

WATCH for changes in your potato. When roots have formed, plant it in soil. Pull off some of the stems that grow out of it. Leave only 3 or 4 of the strongest.

WAIT for the stems to sneak around. Soon you will have a sneaky vine.

Root of the Matter

You have one. How do you get more? With some things it's hard to do. With plants it is pretty easy.

Plant a violet in your yard. Before you know it there are violets everywhere. How did there get to be so many more than before?

A lot of them come from seeds. One plant can make hundreds of seeds. Others come from roots, tubers, corms, and bulbs that get so big in the underground darkness that they divide into pieces. Each piece holds the hope of a new plant.

One leaf is all you need of some plants to make more. Others have to give up a whole piece of their stem to do it.

A few are very cautious. They send out a long thread-like runner to search for a good spot to grow another.

There are so many ways for a plant to propagate. With just a little help there will always be more than before.

portable gardens

Carrot Basket

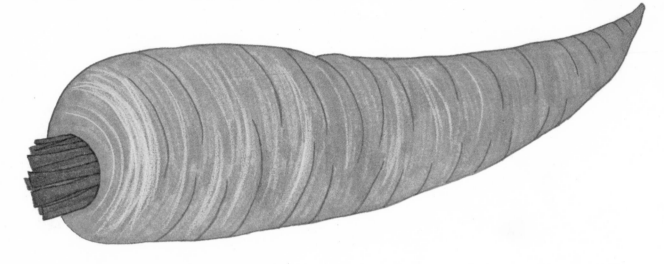

GET a really fat carrot. You probably won't find a monster carrot in a grocery store. So check in a farmer's market or someone's garden. You might want to grow your own

BREAK OFF the leaves. Cut a 3 inch piece from the top of the carrot.

TURN the piece of carrot upside down. Scoop out some of the insides to make a bowl.

OPEN the outside part of a paper clip. Shove the open end into the side of the carrot. Have it 1/2 inch from the cut end.

DO the same thing with 2 more paper clips. Keep the same amount of space between them.

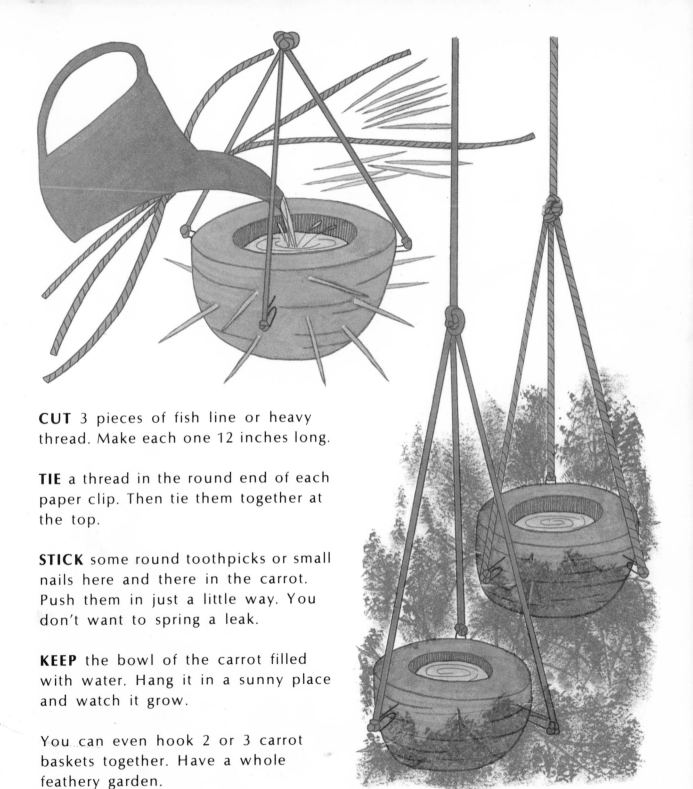

CUT 3 pieces of fish line or heavy thread. Make each one 12 inches long.

TIE a thread in the round end of each paper clip. Then tie them together at the top.

STICK some round toothpicks or small nails here and there in the carrot. Push them in just a little way. You don't want to spring a leak.

KEEP the bowl of the carrot filled with water. Hang it in a sunny place and watch it grow.

You can even hook 2 or 3 carrot baskets together. Have a whole feathery garden.

31

Wet Feet

GROW a planter full of beauties that like keeping their feet wet.

COLLECT four jars the same size. Small peanut butter jars would be good.

BREAK UP some charcoal for the bottom of each jar. This will keep the water clean. Fill the jars with water.

PUT a piece of balsam in one jar, Chinese evergreen in another, coleus in another, and ivy in the last one. Remove any leaves that are below the water.

FIND a box that the jars will fit in without much room to spare. A big shoe box might do the trick. Decorate it so it will make a pretty holder for your watery garden.

ARRANGE the plants the way they look the best to you. Keep them out of the direct sun. Some of them might get sunburned.

FEED them a little liquid plant food once a month. Pinch off straggly branches. Above all, keep their feet wet.

Bashful Basket

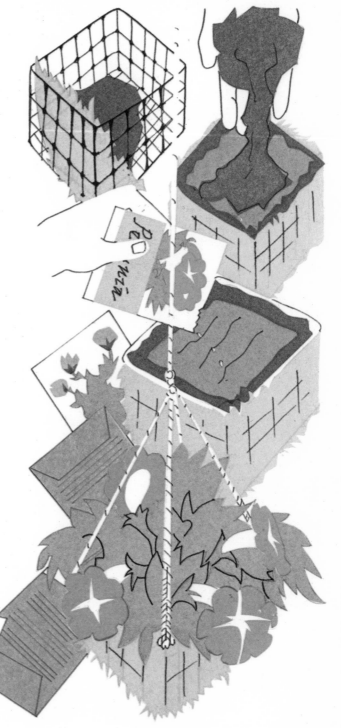

SAVE a plastic vegetable basket. Use the kind that has a lot of holes in it.

LINE the basket with a 1 inch layer of moss. Put the fuzzy part toward the outside.

PUT a 2 inch layer of potting soil in the middle of the moss. Wet it enough to make it damp.

CHOOSE some plants. Try sweet clover, chickweed, petunias, or a begonia. Plant them in the soil.

TIE a piece of heavy string or twine to each corner of the basket. Tie the pieces together at the top. Hook another piece of twine where they join.

HANG your bashful basket outside. Add a drop or two of liquid fertilizer once a month for a treat. Your plants will blush with gratitude.

Herb Ins & Outs

PLAN a year-round herb garden that you can move about, in or out. Herbs are pretty flowering plants and give wonderful flavors to foods.

PLANT a different kind of herb in each pot. Thyme, sage, rosemary, chives, mint, and oregano do well. They are all perennials. That means they grow year after year, all by themselves. You don't have to plant the seeds again, even if you plant them outside.

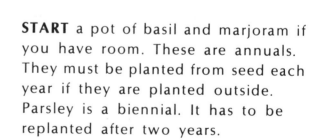

START a pot of basil and marjoram if you have room. These are annuals. They must be planted from seed each year if they are planted outside. Parsley is a biennial. It has to be replanted after two years.

GIVE your potted herbs good care and they will last many seasons. Put the plants outside when the weather is warm enough.

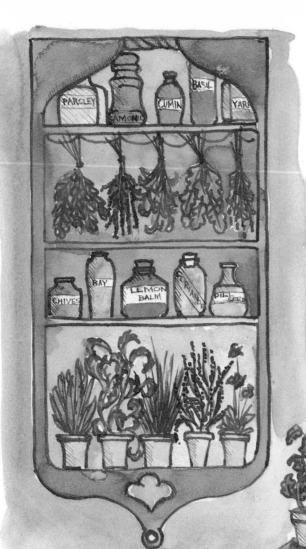

ARRANGE them around your porch or patio for the summer. Set the bottom of the pot in a hole in the ground if you can. They won't dry out as quickly.

SNIP sprigs. Put them in bunches to sell or to give as gifts.

DRY leaves on screens or in tied, hanging bunches. When dry, put them in air-tight containers.

BRING the pots back into your cozy kitchen as soon as the nights get chilly in the fall. Enjoy herbs all winter.

DIVIDE your herb plants when they get too big for their pots. Exchange extras with your friends. Use some to start a permanent herb garden outside. Keep some of each kind for your traveling show, though.

Miniscape

GET a clear glass container with a cover you can take off. A fish bowl, an old aquarium, a brandy snifter, or a large jar will work.

MAKE a cover from plastic wrap or aluminum foil if your container doesn't have one.

PUT a layer of coarse gravel, broken pots or aquarium gravel on the bottom. This will be the drainage material.

MAKE this bottom layer 1 inch deep if you use a small container. Use 2 inches when you use a large container.

USE peat moss or pieces of dead leaves for the next layer. Make this layer thin. You need only enough to keep the soil out of the drainage material.

BREAK some charcoal into chips for the third layer. Use the kind people put in an outdoor grill. Or buy some chips from a garden supply store.

PUT in 2 or 3 handfuls of charcoal. It keeps the soil from smelling sour. It also helps keep it clean.

PUT a layer of soil on the top. Use 4 parts soil to 1 part peat moss.

TRY to get some leaves that microbes have worked on. Mix a handful with the soil and peat moss. They will make good fertilizer.

HAVE the soil layer about 2 inches deep. This will be enough for the roots to grow.

WORK OUT your design before you do any planting. Put taller plants in the back so the shorter ones can be seen. Choose plants that go with the size of your container.

DECIDE whether you want woodland plants or tropical plants. Don't mix them. They need different things and won't grow well together. A seed catalog or florist might give you some ideas.

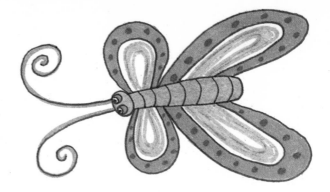

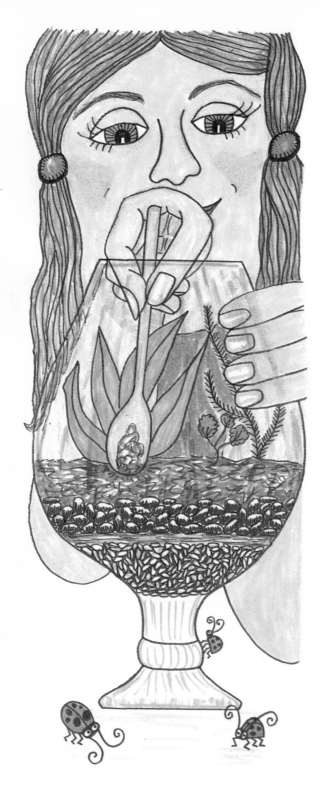

USE plants like ferns, wintergreen, violets, or partridge berry if you decide on a woodland miniscape.

TRY plants such as strawberry begonia, philodendron, ferns, or croton for a tropical miniscape.

SCOOP OUT a hole in the soil for each plant. Make it big enough to hold a ball of soil or cutting.

REMEMBER to space the plants so they have room to grow. Put them far enough from the side to keep them from bumping it as they get bigger.

CARPET the soil with moss if you like. Choose a short moss instead of a long, spongy one. It will last a lot longer.

LET the soil drink by spraying water on your miniscape. You can use an old spray bottle from window cleaner. Be sure you clean it well before you use it.

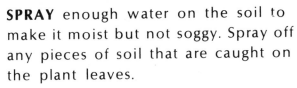

SPRAY enough water on the soil to make it moist but not soggy. Spray off any pieces of soil that are caught on the plant leaves.

WIPE the glass off with a paper tissue. Try not to bump the plants.

PUT ON the cover. Make a small opening to let the air move in and out.

SET your miniscape in a place that has only a little light and is cool. Leave it for 2 days to let it rest. After this rest, the plants will be used to their new home.

MOVE the container to a place that gets a lot of sunlight. But not in direct sunlight.

WATCH your miniscape grow. Wouldn't it be fun to make yourself small enough to visit inside for a day?

Caring Hints

KEEP a woodland miniscape in a cooler room than a tropical one.

WATER your plants once a month with the spray bottle. They will use only a few teaspoonfuls. Don't let your finger get carried away.

SET OUT the water a day before you use it. Leave it overnight to make sure it is room temperature.

WATCH for drops of water on the glass. There should be some moisture just above the soil and on the cover. Drops all over the container mean you gave the plants too much water.

TAKE OFF the cover and wipe off the glass. Do this until most of the drops are gone.

USE an artist's paint brush to clean up any soil that gets on the plant leaves. Brush it off gently.

PULL OFF any dead leaves. Be a neat housekeeper for this small world.

Button Business

GROW a gift for someone you like. Make a teeny, tiny garden.

GET a large coat button. Choose a brightly colored one with a rim around the edge.

LOOK around your yard or in a park for some moss. Or get a tiny piece of bark with moss on it.

GLUE the moss on the button. Find some very small things to put on the moss. Use a toothpick to make a hole for each tiny thing you choose. Put a small drop of glue in each hole.

TRY pieces of lichen, tips of cactus, interesting twigs, or tiny dried flowers. You can even put colored pebbles or shells on your button garden.

ADD a drop of water to the moss if everything begins to look dried out. Handle your teeny, tiny garden carefully. You're about 50 times bigger.

Dunescape

BE BRAVE. Make a garden with a cactus plant or two in it. You will need some ice tongs or a large pair of tweezers. This is going to get prickly.

FIND a container. You can use a planter or a pan with low sides. Or try a glass jar with a wide mouth.

MIX some special soil. Use 1/2 sand, 1/4 potting soil and 1/4 peat moss. Put 2 or 3 inches of soil in your container.

CHOOSE your plants. Use a few tall ones like snake plant, old man cactus, or cereus cactus.

HAVE 1 or 2 medium-sized plants such as panda plant or kalanchoe. Put in 1 or 2 smaller plants. Try hen and chickens or sand dollar.

DRAW your design on paper before you plant anything. Make sure you know where you want to put each plant before you handle it.

MAKE a hole in the soil for each plant. Use the tweezers or tongs to set the cacti in the holes.

SPRINKLE some sand and aquarium gravel on the soil if you want. You can even put in some small rocks or a piece of bleached driftwood. The plants won't need them. But they will make your dunescape look real.

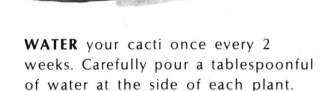

WATER your cacti once every 2 weeks. Carefully pour a tablespoonful of water at the side of each plant.

SET your dunescape in the window every morning. Let the sun shine right on it.

MOVE it somewhere else in the afternoon. The glass makes the sun hotter. Even a cactus can get sunburned.

Mountain Magic

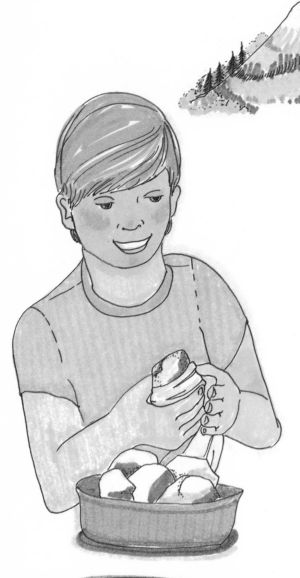

MAKE a miniature garden that looks like a happy place in the mountains.

GET a container with high sides. It will need to be at least 7 inches deep.

PUT a 2 inch layer of broken pots or coarse gravel on the bottom. Spread a 1 inch layer of peat moss on top.

ADD a 1 inch layer of sand next. Fill the container almost to the top with a soil mixture.

USE 2 cups of soil, 2 cups of perlite, and 3 teaspoons of bonemeal. Mix it all together.

LOOK for some soft rocks like shale, sandstone or limestone. Get pieces of concrete blocks or brick if you can't find natural rocks. Break them up with a hammer.

SCRUB the rocks with soap and water. Rinse them off and dry them.

CHOOSE your plants. Use some kind of leafy plant for the background. You might want to try a velvet plant or some kind of fern.

GET 1 or 2 medium-sized plants like phlox, lily of the valley, or pinks. Put in some low vines like smilax, wandering Jew, or cupid vine.

DRAW your design on paper. Then put the rocks in the soil. Tilt them to make your mini-mountains look real.

LET about 1/3 of each rock show. Pat the soil around the rocks.

PUT the plants in next. Remember to space them so they have room to grow. Sprinkle some granite chips on the soil if you have any.

SET your mini-mountains where they will get sun in the morning and evening. Keep the soil damp. Check it often in hot weather.

You'll never climb these mountains. But you can enjoy them a lot.

INDEX

African violet, 15
alkaline soil, 10
Amazing Avocado, 25
balsam, 32
Bashful Basket, 33
basil, 34
Bathing Your Beauties, 11
begonia, 33
Boastful Beet, 23
bone meal, 7
Boston fern, 20
bulbs, 28
Button Business, 41
cactus, 7, 41, 42
Care & Training, 5
Caring Hints, 40
Carrot Basket, 30
cereus cactus, 42
chickweed, 33
Chinese evergreen, 32
chives, 34
clover, sweet, 33
coleus, 32
corms, 28
Crazy Carrot, 22
croton, 38
cupid vine, 45
Cut Offs, 17
dieffenbachia, 18
Dirty Mix-Up, 7
Disappearing Stripes, 15
dried flowers, 41
drip dish, 9
Dunescape, 42
Eggs for Lunch, 10
feeding chart, 40
ferns, 21, 38, 45
gardens, 12
geranium, 17

hen & chickens, 20, 42
Herbs Ins & Outs, 34
ivy, 11, 16, 32
juniper, 19
kalanchoe, 42
lichen, 41
lily of the valley, 45
limestone, 7
Lucky Leaf, 14
marjoram, 34
miniature gardens, 38—45
Miniscape, 36—39
mint, 34
More Than Before, 13
moss, 38—41
Mountain Magic, 44
oregano, 34
Outcast Onion, 26
palms, 11
panda plant, 42
parsley, 34
parsnip, 23
partridge berry, 38
peat moss, 7
perlite, 7
petunias, 33
philodendron, 11, 16, 38
phlox, 45
pinks, 45
plant potting, 6
plant reproduction, 14—28
Pokey Pineapple, 24
Portable Gardens, 29
Pot & Repot, 6
pots, types of, 6
potting soil, 7
Rain Maker, 8
reproduction, 14—28
rex begonia, 14

rhododendron, 19
roots, 28
Root of the Matter, 28
rosemary, 34
rubber plant, 18
runners, 20
sage, 34
sand, 7
sand dollar, 42
seeds, 28
seedlings, 6
Send a Runner, 20
similax, 45
slip (cutting), 16
snake plant, 15, 21, 42
Sneaky Sweet Potato, 27
soil, potting, 7
sphagnum moss, 18
spider plant, 20
sphagnum moss, 18
spider plant, 20
strawberry begonia, 38
strawberry plants, 20
The Great Divide, 21
thyme, 34
Tip Slips, 16
tropical miniscape, 38, 40
tubers, 28
Up In The Air, 18
velvet plant, 45
vermiculture, 7
violets, 28, 38
Violet Vim, 15
volcanic rock, 7
wandering Jew, 16, 45
watering, 8, 9
Wet Feet, 32
wintergreen, 38
woodland miniscape, 38, 40

ILLUSTRATORS

CARE & TRAINING

page   5:   Thomas Petiet
page   6-7:   Bonnie S. Greenwald
page   8-9:   Jacqueline Sharp
page 10-11:   Laura Whitesides Host
page   12:   David LaVerne Laetz

MORE THAN BEFORE

page   13:   Thomas Petiet
page 14-15:   Jan Wentz
page 16-17:   Jacqueline Sharp
page 18-19:   Amy Hill
page 20-21:   Ann G. Clipson
page 22-23:   Rebecca Levenson
page 24-25:   Bonnie S. Greenwald
page 26-27:   Fred G. Baditol
page   28:   David LaVerne Laetz

PORTABLE GARDENS

page   29:   Thomas Petiet
page 30-31:   Laurie Flynn
page 32-33:   Elizabeth Golz Rush
page 34-35:   Martha McCollough
page 36-39:   Nancy W. Abbott
page 40-41:   Rebecca Levenson
page 42-43:   Amy Hill
page 44-45:   Elizabeth MacGregor

About the Editors

Cameron John and Margaret A. Yerian have advanced degrees in psychology and mass communications from the University of Michigan. They have been active in educational and instructional writing for both adults and children, with many publications to their credit. Their work has ranged from the Educational Television Project in American Samoa, where Mrs. Yerian served as a producer/director and Mr. Yerian was a writer and editor to their present work as media consultants in the Detroit metropolitan area.